FIRST
BIOGRAPHIES

Paul Revere

Published by Raintree Steck-Vaughn Publishers, an imprint of Steck-Vaughn Company

Retold for young readers by Edith Vann
Editor: Pam Wells
Project Manager: Julie Klaus
Electronic Production: Scott Melcer

Library of Congress Cataloging-in-Publication Data

Gleiter, Jan, 1947-
    Paul Revere / Jan Gleiter and Kathleen Thompson; [retold for young readers by Edith Vann]; illustrated by Francis Balistreri.
      p.   cm. — (First biographies)
    ISBN 0-8114-8452-1
    1. Revere, Paul, 1735-1818 — Juvenile literature.   2. Statesmen — Massachusetts — Biography — Juvenile literature.   3. Massachusetts — Biography — Juvenile literature.   4. Massachusetts — History — Revolution, 1775-1783 — Juvenile literature.   I. Thompson, Kathleen. II. Balistreri, Francis.   III. Title.   IV. Series.
F69.R43G49   1995
973.3'311'092 — dc20   94-40992
[B]   CIP   AC

Printed and bound in the United States
 2 3 4 5 6 7 8 9 0 W 99 98

FIRST BIOGRAPHIES

Paul Revere

Jan Gleiter and Kathleen Thompson
Illustrated by Francis Balistreri

RSVP

RAINTREE
STECK-VAUGHN
PUBLISHERS

The Steck-Vaughn Company

Austin, Texas

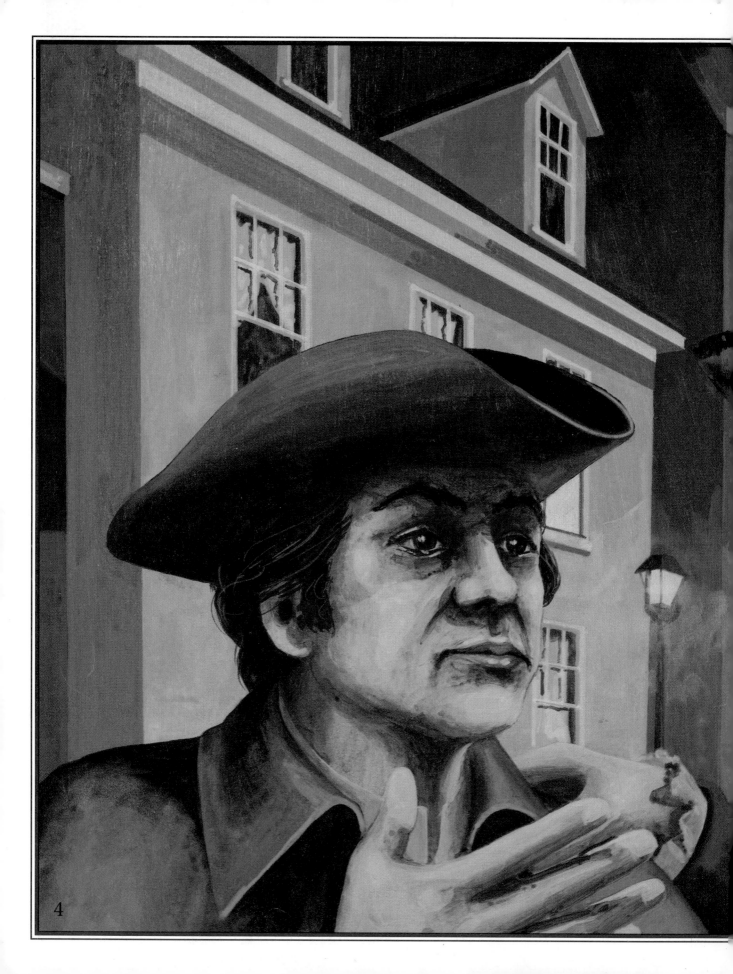

4

"**T**onight the British move," said Dr. Warren.

Paul Revere asked, "By land or by sea?"

"We don't know yet," said Dr. Warren. "But you'll be riding soon."

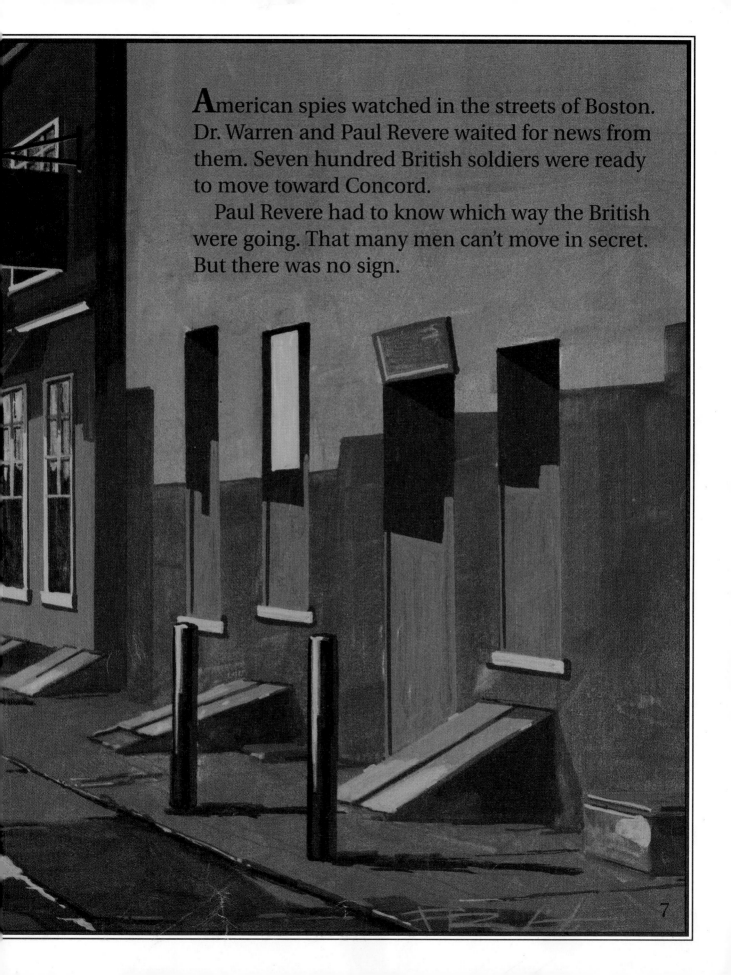

American spies watched in the streets of Boston. Dr. Warren and Paul Revere waited for news from them. Seven hundred British soldiers were ready to move toward Concord.

Paul Revere had to know which way the British were going. That many men can't move in secret. But there was no sign.

The waiting men loved their country. They believed they should be free. There were quarrels between the colonies and the mother country, England. The ties between them were no longer close. These were serious problems.

The colonists hated to pay for the British government. They had no part in it. They wanted to help make their own rules. If the king had listened to them, things might have been different.

This was not Paul's first act in the call to be free.
Two years earlier, in 1773, the British had put a tax on tea. The colonists had to pay it on any tea they bought. They did not think this was fair.

Paul Revere and other colonists dressed as Indians. They climbed on the British East India Tea Company ships. And they threw the tea into Boston Harbor. The tea was worth about $90,000.

King George III was very angry about the Boston Tea Party. So the British made hard new laws. The colonists felt they could not live with these laws.

In 1774 fifty-six men from all the colonies except Georgia met. They talked about what to do. That meeting was later called the First Continental Congress.

13

14

The colonists made up their minds. They would not follow the new British laws. Because of this, the British sent soldiers and ships. Then some colonists trained themselves to fight. They said they could be ready to fight in a minute. So they were called Minutemen.

Everyone in the colonies knew there would be fighting. One of their leaders, Patrick Henry, had said so. He spoke what others were thinking.

He said he did not know what others might do. Then came the words that would ring out across a new nation.

"But as for me, give me liberty or give me death."

War was coming. Perhaps the fighting would begin that night.

17

These brave men had a plan. They would show which way the British were going. Lanterns would be hung in the Old North Church tower. One lantern would be hung if the British went by land. Two lanterns would show if they crossed the Charles River by boat.

At last word came. Two lighted lanterns were hung.

Then Paul Revere crossed the river. He rode his horse hard into the night. He was riding for the life of his country.

"We'll be ready for them," Paul thought. His horse ran on and on. "But they won't be ready for us."

It had to work. It was their only chance. The British had more men and more guns. But no one is braver than a person fighting for home and to be free.

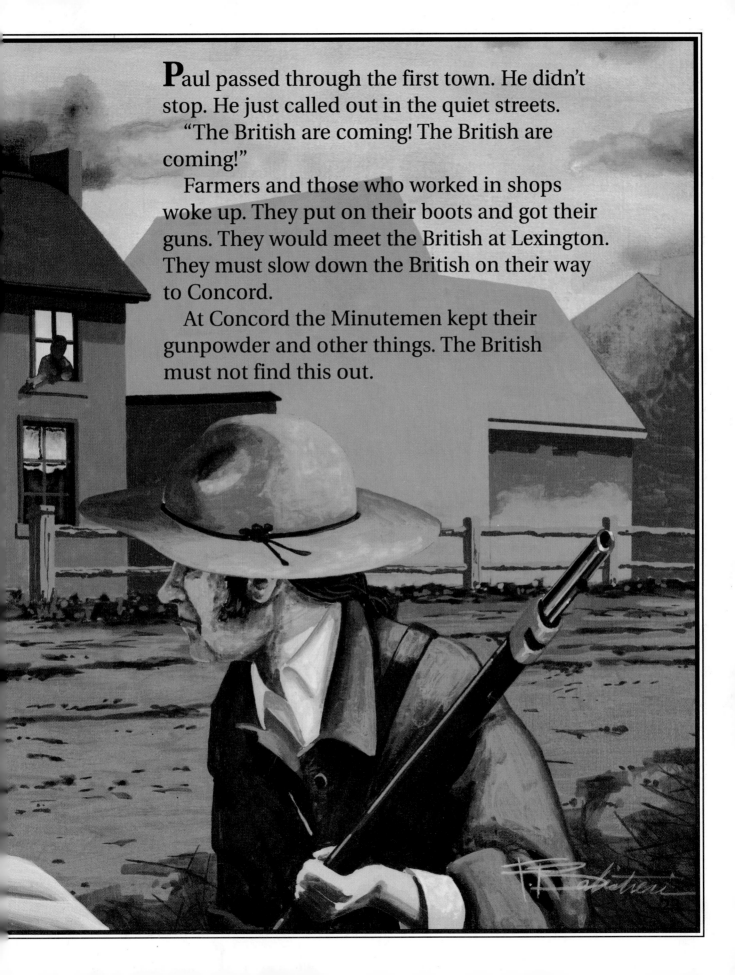

Paul passed through the first town. He didn't stop. He just called out in the quiet streets.

"The British are coming! The British are coming!"

Farmers and those who worked in shops woke up. They put on their boots and got their guns. They would meet the British at Lexington. They must slow down the British on their way to Concord.

At Concord the Minutemen kept their gunpowder and other things. The British must not find this out.

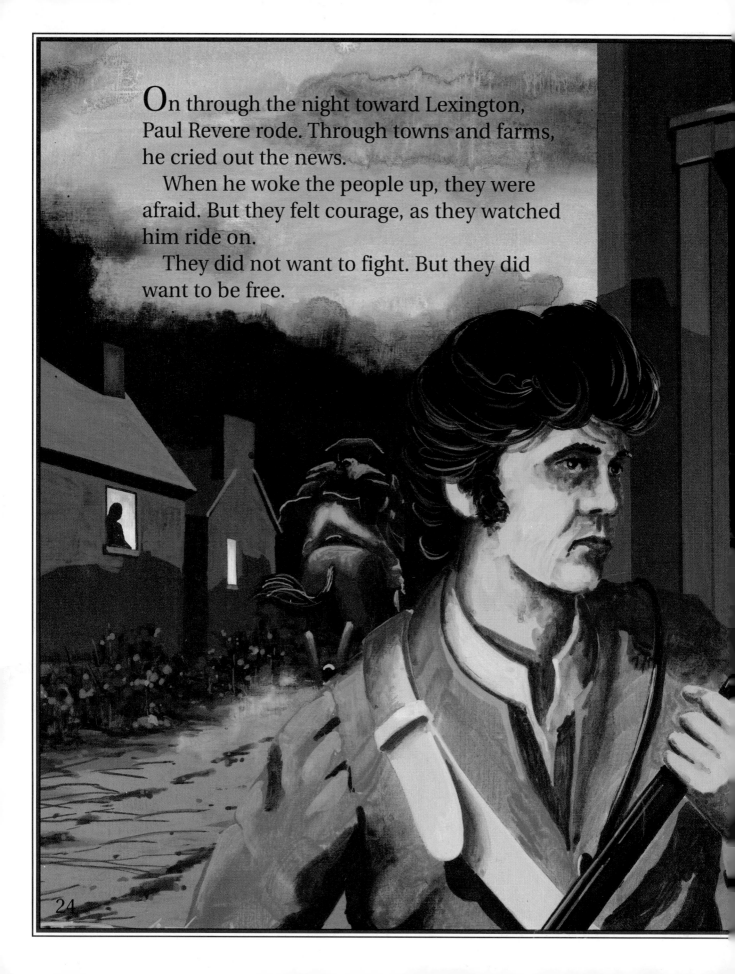

On through the night toward Lexington, Paul Revere rode. Through towns and farms, he cried out the news.

When he woke the people up, they were afraid. But they felt courage, as they watched him ride on.

They did not want to fight. But they did want to be free.

"Faster!" Paul whispered to his horse. "Faster!"

Sam Adams and John Hancock waited at Lexington to hear from him. The British wanted to catch them for working against the king.

Sam Adams had planned the Boston Tea Party. John Hancock had also worked to make America free. These brave men must not be found.

By morning the British reached Lexington. Adams and Hancock had gone. On the Green were fifty Minutemen. The British told them to throw down their guns and go home.

Minuteman Captain Parker told his men, "Don't fire unless you are fired on. But if they want war, let it begin here."

29

The British fired. Eight Minutemen were killed and ten hurt.

The British moved on toward Concord. The Minutemen were waiting. Paul Revere was caught and held a short time. But his friend had made it to Concord.

The British began to look for the gunpowder. Then the "shot heard 'round the world" was fired.

Minutemen fired from behind trees and walls at the British. And the British turned and moved quickly back toward Boston.

That day, April 19, 1775, the American Revolution began.

Key Dates

1735   Paul Revere is born on January 1 in Boston, Massachusetts.

Studies at North Grammar School in Boston.
Learns to be a silversmith.

1756   Paul serves in the French and Indian War.

1757   Marries Sarah Orne.
Works in his father's business as a silversmith.
Creates political cartoons.

1773   Sarah Orne dies. Paul marries Rachel Walker.

Dumps boxes of tea into Boston harbor on the night of December 16.

1775   Rides to Lexington, April 18. Warns other brave Americans that the British are coming. The British capture Revere and later release him on foot.

1776   Builds a powder mill at Canton, Massachusetts.

1778-1779   Commands a fort in Boston Harbor.

1779   Serves as a commander in Maine.

1780   Goes back to being a silversmith again.

1818   Paul Revere dies in Boston on May 10.

Note: Henry Wadsworth Longfellow's poem "Paul Revere's Ride" places Paul Revere in Concord on April 19, 1775. However, after he warned the patriots in Lexington, he was captured by the British and did not reach Concord.